# Papers

by

## Allan Stratton

SAMUEL FRENCH, INC.

45 WEST 25TH STREET NEW YORK 10010
7623 SUNSET BOULEVARD HOLLYWOOD 90046
*LONDON* *TORONTO*

ISBN 0 573 69146 0 Printed in U.S.A.

*This play is dedicated to Urjo Kareda*

*Special thanks to Joseph Byers, Craig Shipler, Gordon Floyd & Dorothy and Alex McPhedran.*

## IMPORTANT BILLING AND CREDIT REQUIREMENTS

All producers of PAPERS *must* give credit to the Author of the Play in all programs distributed in connection with performances of the Play and in all instances in which the title of the Play appears for purposes of advertising, publicizing or otherwise exploiting the Play and/or a production. The name of the Author *must* also appear on a separate line, on which no other name appears, immediately following the title, and *must* appear in size of type not less than fifty percent the size of the title type.

*PAPERS* was first produced at the Tarragon Theatre, Toronto, on November 26, 1985 with the following cast:

MYRA............. Patricia Hamilton
CHARLES ........ Les Carlson
BOBBI............. Alison Lawrence

Directed by Stephen Katz
Sets and costumes by Iain Aitken
Lighting by Jim Plaxton
Stage Managed by Bruce McKinnon

## CHARACTERS

Myra Fitzpatrick (Moira)
Charles Martin
Bobbi Roy

## SETTING

The front room of a university guest home.*

## TIME

The present.

---

* In ACT II the back wall divides and a simple office dolly unit rolls in.

## ACT I

*SCENE: A spotlight rises Downstage Right.*

*AT RISE: Professor MOIRA FITZSIMMONS stands behind a lectern in academic gown. SHE addresses the audience.*

MOIRA. No, I am not embarrassed. No, I am not angry. No, I am not betrayed. I am, however, tired of repeating that to everyone from check-out attendants at Loblaws to Robert Fulford and Barbara Frum. Which is why I have decided to devote today's public lecture to *Papers*, the new novel by my friend, Martin Edwards. Martin Edwards, last year's Writer-In-Residence here at Lakeside, has set his tale in the university town of *Lakeview*. His central characters are a novelist, Charles Martin, and a neurotic academic, Myra Fitzpatrick. That my name is Moira has added spice to every dinner party I haven't attended. But Martin's gift for subtlety notwithstanding, *Papers* is fiction. Let us begin by studying his opening paragraphs. (*Reads.*) "Charles Martin had spent the day grinning like a moron at an endless stream of intellectual toads, known as the academic faculty."

(*There is a cross-fade, with LIGHTS coming up on the front room of Charles Martin's university–furnished home. It's not designed for hangovers: floral wallpaper, linoleum, knick-knack shelves and Stage Right a bar with a Hawaii motif – fishnets and shellfish. Sitting on the bar is a recently acquired case of scotch, open. Up from the bar is a door to the interior. The front door is Stage Left, a writing desk down from it, on which is a typewriter, desk lamp, typing paper and a small sculpture of Buddha, for luck. CHARLES, who could use some luck, is just in the process of moving in, which accounts for several half-unpacked boxes and suitcases. As the LIGHTS rise HE is slumped Centre Stage on the couch. He has clearly had a trying day. A large scotch sits on the table in front of him.*)

MOIRA. (*Reading.*) "They had provided him with a furnished home. Sort of. Their notion of an upscale garret. At least there was peace and quiet."

(*There is a knock on the front door.*)

MOIRA. (*Reading.*) "Except for the knock on the door."

CHARLES. Damn.

MOIRA. (*Reading.*) "Never mind. He would put his rage on ice. For the moment."

(*LIGHT is now completely off MOIRA, who disappears. There is another knock on the front door.*)

CHARLES. Coming. (*Downs his scotch and goes to the front door. HE looks in the mirror, tries to straighten his hair, and forces a social smile. Another knock.*) Yes.

(*CHARLES opens front door to find MYRA (Moira) standing outside. SHE is middle-aged, in a cloth coat; attractive and crisp.*)

## ACT I

### Scene 1

MYRA. Welcome to Lakeview Mr. Martin. It's home to us. We hope it will be home to you.

CHARLES. (*A little too charming.*) Are you the Welcome Wagon?

MYRA. Professor Fitzpatrick. Call me Myra.

CHARLES. Ah yes. Who wrote the charming invitation.

MYRA. On behalf of the faculty. And you're Charles Martin who writes uncommonly good fiction. And I am not given to compliments.

CHARLES. Glad you enjoy it.

MYRA. Enjoy it. I teach it. May I come in?

CHARLES. The place is a mess.

MYRA. I don't mind. (*Enters, removing her coat.*) I just had to see how you were getting along.

CHARLES. I'm unpacking.

MYRA. Then I won't stay a minute.

CHARLES. Fine.

MYRA. Good. (*Holds her coat out.*)

CHARLES. (*Making no move to take it.*) Nice coat.

MYRA. It's cloth.

CHARLES. Nice cloth. (*Takes it.*)

MYRA. It's given good wear. But enough small talk, I'm delighted you're here.

CHARLES. My pleasure.

MYRA. I wanted to speak to you after your lecture this afternoon. But the reception was so packed, so pressed, and everywhere I turned people were breathing on me and I – I – well I thought, "Myra, if you don't get out of here you're going to embarrass yourself."

CHARLES. You hate crowds?

MYRA. I hate students.

CHARLES. But you must love teaching.

MYRA. I *loathe* teaching. I love *research.* But to return to your lecture. I enjoyed it enormously, from my aisle seat by the exit.

CHARLES. Glad you were entertained.

MYRA. I wasn't. I was engaged. "The Nuclear Artist: Secular Priest or Merchant of Dreams."

CHARLES. Wretched title.

MYRA. (*Looking around.*) Provocative. And delivered with such control, such authority, such élan.

(*CHARLES has Myra's coat at the front closet. There are no hangers. HE tosses her coat on the floor and closes the door, unnoticed, as MYRA continues to speak.*)

MYRA. In fact you were exactly like – well not what the faculty expected, thank God – but exactly what we hoped for.

CHARLES. What do you mean?

MYRA. You were professional.

CHARLES. Pardon?

MYRA. Sober. Please don't misunderstand. But when it comes to drinking you writers stagger the imagination: In fact when it comes to drinking you stagger generally.

CHARLES. It comes from having to talk to strangers with opinions.

MYRA. No need to be defensive. Writers need to experience everything that life has to offer. It's all grist for the mill.

CHARLES. (*Tight smile.*) Spoken like a trouper. Drink?

MYRA. Please. Sherry with a twist.

CHARLES. (*Points to case of scotch.*) Scotch?

MYRA. Fine. (*As CHARLES heads for drinks.*) But a Writer-in-Residence is also an example to the student body. And frankly, a Governor General's Award winner half-naked in the fountain vomiting is not a pretty sight. It shakes one's faith in culture.

CHARLES. Not to mention drunks. Who was it?

MYRA. Albert Fennig. We barely kept his name out of the papers.

CHARLES. For throwing up on campus?

MYRA. For being indiscreet in public washrooms.

CHARLES. Oh.

MYRA. Not that he wasn't experiencing grist for his mill. I'm sure he was. But the trouble is, most students don't put such conduct in perspective. They look at an Albert Fennig and say, "If I want to be a great author like Albert Fennig all I have to do is commit unspeakable acts in a public place," And art just isn't that simple. If it were, we academics would be out of work and you could kiss Varsity fundraising goodbye!

CHARLES. Bravo!

MYRA. Forgive me. I get on one of my hobby horses and I start to lecture. It's an occupational hazard.

CHARLES. Next time I'll take notes.

MYRA. Sorry.

CHARLES. Don't be sorry. Glad to see you're 'engaged.' (*Hands her scotch.*) Cheers.

MYRA. Cheers. At any rate, that's why your lecture was wonderful. You proved you belonged. In fact you passed with flying colours.

CHARLES. I didn't realize it was a test.

MYRA. A trial. At least for me. I sponsored you in committee. Put my credibility on the line. But you came through. And you even had something to say.

CHARLES. You sound surprised.

MYRA. Oh *I* wasn't. But I don't mind admitting, getting your name through committee was an ordeal. You can understand why.

CHARLES. (*Icy smile.*) No. Perhaps you'd like to tell me.

MYRA. I'm afraid my colleagues take writing seriously.

CHARLES. So do I.

MYRA. That's fortunate, you being a novelist. But when I say seriously I mean 'seriously.' Unfortunately you're funny.

CHARLES. Oh yes. And feeling funnier by the minute.

MYRA. I'm not being clear.

CHARLES. (*Tight smile.*) On the contrary. Clarity is the least of your problems. (*Downs rest of his drink and goes for another.*)

MYRA. You misunderstand. Your work's witty, original and observant. But my colleagues consider humour beneath them. Having devoted their lives to ideas they're looking for depth.

CHARLES. I have depth.

MYRA. Of course you do. But jokes don't resonate.

CHARLES. I don't write jokes. I write character in situation. If that's funny, tough. It's the truth.

MYRA. Absolutely. The human comedy. That's what I argued in committee. And as you can see I won because here you are.

CHARLES. Am I supposed to be grateful?

MYRA. I'm not sure. Aren't you?

CHARLES. I'm polite.

MYRA. (*Awkward beat.*) I can't tell you how much I appreciate you inviting me in like this. I can see we're going to be great friends.

(*CHARLES' eyes glaze, though the smile remains fixed. Beat.*)

MYRA. Hello?

CHARLES. Yes?

MYRA. Your eyes went blank.

CHARLES. Sorry.

MYRA. You were thinking, weren't you?

CHARLES. I hope so.

MYRA. Taking mental notes, I'll bet. This is going to end up in a book.

CHARLES. It is?

MYRA. Of course. You writers are like squirrels. You store up the people you meet as if we were nuts. (*Beat.*) Perhaps I should rephrase that.

CHARLES. Not at all. (*Looks for a pen to write down her line.*)

MYRA. I have a pen.

CHARLES. Thanks.

MYRA. (*As she gives it to him.*) How exciting. To be a fragment in a book. To be organized into art. Do you think I'm a crank?

CHARLES. Why do you ask?

MYRA. Because I suspect that dreary Mr. Freud would call me repressed. And I'm not. I'm simply very straightforward and a lot of people find that frightening. It's why I've never married.

CHARLES. Pardon?

MYRA. I won't be a Kewpie Doll. For anyone. Why should I be expected to 'ooh' and 'ahh' over a blind date named Fred who's never heard of Melville, Hawthorne or dental floss? What are you looking at?

CHARLES. Forgive me, but do you always carry on conversations like this?

MYRA. You think I'm coming on too strong?

CHARLES. No, no. It's just that I don't talk a lot.

MYRA. I noticed. You writers are astonishingly quiet when you're not drunk.

CHARLES. (*Pouring himself another.*) As I was saying, I don't talk a lot. So when I meet someone who does I'm curious.

MYRA. You *do* think I'm a crank.

CHARLES. You talk in monologues.

MYRA. Only because everyone I know is very quiet. I talk to break up the silences.

CHARLES. You don't need to defend yourself.

MYRA. Your remark about monologues was a compliment?

CHARLES. It's just that you're volunteering personal information to a complete stranger.

MYRA. But you're not a stranger. I've read your books.

CHARLES. (*Blankly.*) You've read my books.

MYRA. Several times. And written on them. I've studied your mind. I know how you think. Oh no. Oh dear.

CHARLES. What?

MYRA. I see what you mean. I know all about you but you don't have a clue about me. I'm so sorry. You must think I'm a loon.

CHARLES. Not at all. I'm often confused with my books.

MYRA. That's very gracious but I've talked enough. Your turn.

CHARLES. What?

MYRA. Say something.

CHARLES. I don't know what to say.

MYRA. You see? When I don't talk there's silence!!

CHARLES. But I'm happy taking notes.

MYRA. Look, I may treat people as audiences. But I don't treat them as research and then insult them.

CHARLES. I'm sorry.

MYRA. Never mind. I have an idea. Small talk.

CHARLES. I'm not sure I'm up for it.

MYRA. Just a little mindless chatter to get acquainted.

CHARLES. As long as it's mindless.

MYRA. Very. How do you do, Mr. Martin. I'm Professor Fitzpatrick. Call me Myra.

CHARLES. How do you do Myra. I'm Mr. Martin. Call me Charles.

MYRA. I must say, we're making very good progress, Charles. Don't you think?

CHARLES. Oh yes, Myra. Indeed I do. Drink?

MYRA. That would be lovely.

CHARLES. Lovely.

(*CHARLES pours them drinks. Pause. MYRA smiles, awkwardly struggling for a topic.*)

MYRA. I'll bet you never thought you'd end up here.

CHARLES. You're right.

MYRA. (*Beat.*) Well, it's a pleasure having you.

CHARLES. It's a pleasure being had.

MYRA. (*Pause.*) What do you think of the campus?

CHARLES. It's very green.

MYRA. In winter it's white.

CHARLES. You don't say.

MYRA. Really. (*Beat, indicating room.*) I hope you enjoy the house.

CHARLES. Oh yes. I'm fond of linoleum.

MYRA. It belonged to Professor Marker. Not much of a decorator, I'm afraid.

CHARLES. He's on sabbatical?

MYRA. He's dead.

CHARLES. Oh.

MYRA. But his spirit lives on.

CHARLES. (*Beat, indicating bar with fishnet and starfish motif.*) Did he enjoy Hawaii?

MYRA. He didn't enjoy anything. (*Beat.*) My God, small talk is difficult.

CHARLES. Like life.

MYRA. What?

CHARLES. It's a constant struggle to fill time.

MYRA. That's bleak.

CHARLES. Sorry. Small talk makes me uncomfortable.

MYRA. But the point of small talk isn't to be comfortable. It's to be casual.

CHARLES. I'm not very good at being casual either.

MYRA. We have so much in common.

CHARLES. What? Being socially inept?

MYRA. Socially independent. Not to mention our mutual involvement in language, literature and Lakeview.

CHARLES. Of course. The three 'l's.

MYRA. You don't sound enthused.

CHARLES. Forgive me. I'm having an off decade.

MYRA. Anything I can do to help?

CHARLES. I don't think so. I've just been overcome by one of my moods.

MYRA. Oh. So you're in "the throes", are you?

CHARLES. The what?

MYRA. The throes of artistic creation.

CHARLES. No. As a matter of fact I'm in the throes of realizing I've made a very serious mistake.

MYRA. What about?

CHARLES. I should never have come here.

MYRA. Pardon?

CHARLES. How to put this delicately. Do you enjoy theatre?

MYRA. Yes.

CHARLES. Concerts?

MYRA. Yes.

CHARLES. Restaurants, bistros and delis?

MYRA. Yes.

CHARLES. Well guess what.

MYRA. What?

CHARLES. THEY'RE NOT HERE!!! This is a wasteland, Myra! A WASTELAND!!! It's not for grownups! It's for middle class adolescents on the make! For anyone over twenty-one there's nothing but bowling and bingo!!!

MYRA. It's not the end of the world.

CHARLES. No. But you can see it from here!! I'm sorry. I shouldn't be rude. But I've been smiling all day and my cheeks ache. And now, if you'll excuse me, I think I'll pour myself a long, hot bath, stick my head under water and scream!

MYRA. Was it something I said?

CHARLES. No, it was something I drank. I'm suffocating. Drowning. Dying.

MYRA. Lakeview can do that. My first year was a horror. I vividly remember how depressed I got the first day I realized that what appeared to be bleak and desolate actually was.

CHARLES. And we're trapped!!

MYRA. No! The God-awful desperate emptiness of this place is its chief attraction.

CHARLES. Are you crazy?

MYRA. We're free to think. In an atmosphere with no, and I mean *absolutely* no, distractions.

CHARLES. (*Sarcastic.*) Terrific. I'm so happy. I mean let's run out and buy postcards.

MYRA. You have to look on the bright side.

CHARLES. I'm looking on the bright side and it makes me want to slit my wrists.

MYRA. Charles, depression may be great for inspiration but it makes for one hell of a life.

CHARLES. So does delusion. How am I supposed to think when I've gone out of my mind from boredom?

MYRA. But how could you be bored? Lakeview provides a community of scholars.

CHARLES. Hooray! A reason to live!

MYRA. You're among friends.

CHARLES. Friends? I'm not among friends. I'm among pompous little pinheads who think I'm a joke. Fatuous doughheads! Gasbags with an irony factor of minus ten! Boneheads! They're boneheads! They want significance! Well once your little peabrain figures out you're going to end up rotting in the ground, being significant doesn't seem quite so significant anymore. Oh God I can't stand it! They think I'm funny! Funny!!! Well I am not funny! I am suicidal!!!

MYRA. I should never have mentioned the committee.

CHARLES. Why not? They're my pals. My buddies.

MYRA. I'm sorry.

CHARLES. Don't be. I understand. I have intellectual herpes! They're 'into' ideas and I'm this village idiot who cracks jokes! They're profoundly 'serious' and I'm this baboon who doesn't know how to resonate! I don't offer a showcase for academic ego so I get dismissed as trivial. Well tough! I don't need the art priesthood to intercede with my readers! I don't need any of you!!!

MYRA. You mustn't take it personally.

CHARLES. How else can I take it? When you attack my work you attack *me*.

MYRA. But *I* don't attack you.

CHARLES. No. You demean me. You pat my head for talking to alumni, for being a student role model. To hear you tell it, my central qualification to be here is that I don't throw up in public!

MYRA. That's not true.

CHARLES. It is. You don't want a Writer-in-Residence. You want *Mister Rogers Goes to College*.

MYRA. I want Charles Martin. The author of novels like *Delphi Express*.

CHARLES. That's very kind. But let's not kid ourselves.

MYRA. I don't kid about work.

CHARLES. What work?

MYRA. You were taking notes about me. Well I've been writing a book about you. *Charles Martin And the Post-Modernist Dialectic.*

CHARLES. Pardon?

MYRA. I started last May.

CHARLES. You're analyzing *me*???

MYRA. I have a pet theory. It's very compelling.

CHARLES. I'm too young to be pigeon-holed!!

MYRA. You're forty-nine.

CHARLES. I'm too young to be forty-nine!!!

MYRA. But not too young to have left a substantial body of work.

CHARLES. Left?? I'm not dead!!

MYRA. Sorry. But it *has* been seven years since you published.

CHARLES. Six and who's counting.

MYRA. In academe it's publish or perish.

CHARLES. Novels aren't something you can whip off in an afternoon.

MYRA. Six years isn't an afternoon. And given your previous pace – twelve novels in twelve years, the first four successful –

CHARLES. It's been a while. But that doesn't mean I've stopped.

MYRA. I didn't say you had.

CHARLES. You implied.

MYRA. Sorry.

CHARLES. I've been working hard. Very hard. And the other eight were good.

MYRA. I didn't say they weren't.

CHARLES. They were *very* good. Terrific! Great!

MYRA. Absolutely. What's it called?

CHARLES. What?

MYRA. The new book.

CHARLES. *Papers*.

MYRA. Papers?

CHARLES. Yeah.

MYRA. May I read it?

CHARLES. Not till it's done.

MYRA. When will that be?

CHARLES. When it's done.

MYRA. I can't wait. In the meantime ...

CHARLES. (*Tight.*) Yes?

MYRA. Since you're here, and looking for things to do, would you mind if we set up some interviews?

CHARLES. (*Pause.*) That's why you pushed to get me here, isn't it? It wasn't because of *my* work. It was for yours.

MYRA. Your work is my work.

CHARLES. I don't do interviews.

MYRA. Charles, I'm sorry if I patronized. I'm sorry if I offended.

CHARLES. I'm sorry too. But that's life.

MYRA. Please reconsider. You could help me. But I could also help you. I want to give your work credentials. Respect. It's very dense.

CHARLES. It's garbage.

MYRA. No!

CHARLES. Ask the clones in the faculty lounge. I haven't published in six years. I haven't had a success in fourteen. Out of print is out of mind and I'm down the toilet.

MYRA. If that were true I wouldn't be writing my book.

CHARLES. Why not? Isn't there a market for riches to rags stories? For years they called me a hack and I said I was an artist. But here I am. Smiling at the vermin who attacked me.

Whoring for respect in the halls of academe. Pretty funny for a sellout.

MYRA. It's not funny. You're not a sellout. And I intend to do everything I can to prove it. Please help me.

CHARLES. (*Sad and scared.*) Myra, can I ask you something?

MYRA. What?

CHARLES. Do you really like my work?

MYRA. It's very sharp. Ironic. At its core a magnificent sense of discrepant awareness.

CHARLES. But do you *like* it?

MYRA. (*Simply.*) Yes.

CHARLES. (*Pause.*) Thank you. Thank you. Oh God, Myra, let's have another drink.

MYRA. To *Papers*.

CHARLES. To *The Post-Modernist Dialectic.*

MYRA. And last, but not least, to your stay at Lakeview!

(*CHARLES blanches, downs his scotch.*)

**BLACKOUT**

## ACT I

### Scene Two

*Several months have passed since Scene One. MYRA is interviewing Charles. SHE turns on her tape recorder.*

CHARLES. So what is *The Post-Modernist Dialectic?*

MYRA. It's a secret.

CHARLES. You've been asking mine all fall.

MYRA. This is different. It could mean a major fellowship.

CHARLES. I have a right to know.

MYRA. Charles, my colleagues are vultures. Intellectual magpies. I'm sorry. I can't tell anyone.

CHARLES. Then no more interviews.

MYRA. Charles ...

(*CHARLES stares at her, smiling, lips tightly sealed.*)

MYRA. Okay. But you mustn't breathe a word.

CHARLES. May I be struck dead.

MYRA. *The Post-Modernist Dialectic.* (*Turns off the tape recorder. Then, very conspiratorially, as if the walls have ears, SHE speaks.)*

MYRA. T.S. Eliot's belief in the objective correlative, the artist separate from the art, conflicts with theories which maintain art is the direct communication of the artist's life and emotion. This conflict is what I term the Post-Modernist Dialectic. Your work, on the surface direct and accessible but informed by tight intellectual constructs, is a paradigm of this dialectic.

CHARLES. (*Beat.*) I should never have asked.

MYRA. I'm serious.

CHARLES. I'm impressed. (*Heads for a drink.*)

MYRA. Take your image patterns. The use of cutlery in *Sing Me Gentle,* for instance. The brutal Frank whose mind 'cuts like a knife'; his wife Harriet whose face, chin reaching to touch forehead, resembles 'the inside of a spoon'; or their son Harold, a pathological liar with a tongue metaphorically 'forked'. Ordinary implements transformed; our lives objectified by the instruments of daily life; our secrets, the skeletons in our closets, tumbling out of kitchen drawers and cupboards. Masterful. At once comic and horrifying.

CHARLES. Aren't I a clever boy.

MYRA. You can't tell me that's accidental.

CHARLES. I can't remember.

MYRA. You're too modest.

CHARLES. You're too generous.

MYRA. I'm accurate. But to return to the interview. (*Re-starts tape recorder and consults her notes.*) What do you take to be the central metaphor connecting the internal realities of your characters to their external circumstances?

CHARLES. Is that a trick question?

MYRA. I'm not kidding.

CHARLES. You should be.

MYRA. Don't make fun of me.

CHARLES. I can't help it. Can't we just talk?

MYRA. "Talk?"

CHARLES. You know. Like people.

MYRA. Why would we want to do that?

CHARLES. Because my brain hurts. Let's have fun.

MYRA. I don't enjoy "fun." To me it's a very mysterious concept – like algebra. What's wrong with these questions?

CHARLES. They're wacko.

MYRA. They're academic.

CHARLES. Exactly. They have nothing to do with *how* I write, *why* I write.

MYRA. But my interest is *what* you write.

CHARLES. Really? Judging by your interpretations, what I write and what you read are two different things.

MYRA. On the contrary. What you write and what you *think* you write are two different things.

CHARLES. I think I'm getting angry.

MYRA. When struck for an idea, get mad. How typically male.

CHARLES. AAAAAAAA!!!

MYRA. Feel better?

CHARLES. You can be so infuriating.

MYRA. And you can be so trivial.

CHARLES. Theory is trivial. Not people. Not us.

MYRA. Who said anything about us?

CHARLES. That's why you're here.

MYRA. I'm here to work.

CHARLES. Give me a break.

MYRA. Give *me* a break. You agreed to be interviewed out of self-interest. Period.

CHARLES. Myra, I enjoy your company. Without you, I'd have jumped off the town pier in September.

MYRA. That's very cruel.

CHARLES. What?

MYRA. I know when I'm being laughed at. I better go.

CHARLES. It's the truth. You make me think.

MYRA. Is this a scene for one of your books?

CHARLES. You really care about my work. Do you know what it means to have someone care about your work?

MYRA. (*The answer is really 'no'.*) I think so.

CHARLES. And your opinion matters.

MYRA. (*Nervous laugh.*) I don't know what to say.

CHARLES. How about, "Let's turn off the tape and be friends."

MYRA. (*Smiles, awkwardly, shyly.*) All right. Let's turn off the tape ... and be friends. (*Turns off tape and looks up at Charles. Pause.*)

CHARLES. (*Steady smile.*) Drink?

MYRA. Is this a come on?

CHARLES. Not if the answer's no.

MYRA. (*Pause, carefully.*) Oh. (*Pause.*) A drink might be nice.

(*CHARLES goes to make her a drink.*)

MYRA. You really care about my opinion?

CHARLES. Even when it drives me crazy.

MYRA. Thank you. Thanks ... How's *Papers* coming?

CHARLES. I'm very excited. Finished a chapter this afternoon.

MYRA. I can't wait to read it.

CHARLES. You will. (*Hands her a drink.*) Sherry with a twist.

MYRA. Oh. (*Beat.*) I enjoy our evenings too. They've been the most exciting thing to happen to me in years.

CHARLES. Don't forget your social life.

MYRA. They *are* my social life.

CHARLES. I'm sorry.

MYRA. I'm not. I don't need people. In fact I consider the need to be needed unhealthy. Don't you?

CHARLES. Not when I'm alone at night in a ratty bathrobe staring at my bookshelves. Then I can think of lots of things worse than needing to be needed.

MYRA. Name one.

CHARLES. Sitting alone in a ratty bathrobe staring at my bookshelves.

MYRA. So don't stare. Read.

CHARLES. That can get lonely too. Alone.

MYRA. Not half as lonely as pretending to love someone you don't even like.

CHARLES. There isn't anyone?

MYRA. Eligible bachelors don't flock to Lakeview. And I can't picture myself angling for widowers down at the sawmill.

CHARLES. But at the university –

MYRA. The number of single, heterosexual men over forty is depressing. Those that exist you don't want to meet. Thank God I'm self-sufficient. Always have been.

CHARLES. "Always"? As in "ALWAYS"?

MYRA. Well ...

CHARLES. Aha! A "well"!

MYRA. Well of course there's a "well." You don't have to talk about your past to have one.

CHARLES. Was it dark and dirty? Cast of thousands?

MYRA. Charles!

CHARLES. Just giving you the benefit of the doubt.

MYRA. (*Beat.*) If you must know his name was Robert.

CHARLES. Robert what?

MYRA. Byers. Robert Byers.

CHARLES. And?

MYRA. (*Sharp.*) And that's all. It was before I came here. You don't know him. And it's not for gossip. So leave me alone.

CHARLES. (*Backing away.*) Fine, fine.

MYRA. I'm sorry. It's just that I'm not comfortable discussing ... my personal life. It makes it cheap.

CHARLES. I understand.

MYRA. Robert was very special.

CHARLES. I'm sorry it ended badly.

MYRA. I didn't say that.

CHARLES. You didn't have to.

MYRA. As a matter of fact we were going to get married.

CHARLES. But you didn't.

MYRA. We couldn't. Something came up. Something happened and he, uh, he got very sick. And, well, I'm afraid he never got better.

CHARLES. Forgive me. I really *am* sorry.

MYRA. Why? It's not your fault. It would be nice if life could be arranged like books. But it can't. We don't get what we deserve. We get what we get. That may not be fair. But it's clear. And fine by me. I'd rather eat alone than with somebody else, wishing it was him. Who do you eat with?

CHARLES. I don't eat.

MYRA. Ever?

CHARLES. Maybe a can of fruit cocktail. I like food you can pour.

MYRA. That isn't healthy.

CHARLES. Can't help it. When I'm alone I forget.

MYRA. I could join you.

CHARLES. I have terrible manners. I'd make you sick.

MYRA. I can cope with a lot.

CHARLES. So could my wife. But I have an amazing capacity to disgust.

MYRA. Even your wife?

CHARLES. Especially my wife. It's why she left me.

MYRA. Because of your manners?

CHARLES. No. My manner. *Her* I made sick on principle. So sick she stopped eating with me. And when *she* did, so did *I*.

MYRA. But she left twenty years ago!

CHARLES. How time flies.

MYRA. And you haven't eaten since then?

CHARLES. Oh I eat when I'm having an affair. But I'm lucky if they last through breakfast.

MYRA. That's sordid.

CHARLES. That's life. My wife was the only one to put up with me at all. She deserves a Survival Badge!

MYRA. Her name was Sylvia, wasn't it?

CHARLES. Yes it was. I suspect it still is. She left before I was published. Said she was tired of living like an undergraduate. So was I, but I was a writer. She said that wasn't her problem. She had a point. At any rate she didn't understand me. And I didn't understand her. It was like a contest to see who could understand the other the least. She won.

MYRA. And she just left?

CHARLES. Well not quite. She packed first. Sylvia was very practical. She realized early on that starving in a garret is less fun than eating out. What she didn't realize is that writing isn't something I *decided* to do. It's something I *had* to do. It's a compulsion! An obsession! An addiction! No one should have to live with me.

MYRA. But you get on so well with people.

CHARLES. Oh yes. I'm terrific with people. It's individuals I have problems with. They take it personally when I start mouthing invisible paragraphs when they're talking. In fact, I only have one relationship that matters to me.

MYRA. Who is she?

CHARLES. I'd rather not say.

(*There is a KNOCK on the front door.*)

MYRA. Why not?

CHARLES. It's a secret. Just a sec.

(*CHARLES answers the door. Bobbi Roy, an attractive eighteen year-old is standing outside. She has a file folder of poems.*)

BOBBI. Hi.

CHARLES. Hi.

BOBBI. (*Seeing Myra.*) Am I interrupting something?

CHARLES. I'm being interviewed. For a book.

BOBBI. No kidding. What's it about?

MYRA. *Charles Martin And The Post-Modernist Dialectic.*

BOBBI. Sounds like fun.

CHARLES. Professor Fitzpatrick, Bobbi Roy. Bobbi Roy, Professor Fitzpatrick.

MYRA. We've met.

BOBBI. English 101. Well I guess you're busy. Won't keep you. Just wanted to drop off some stuff. (*Hands Charles the folder of poems.*)

CHARLES. Thanks. Oh wait. How did your weekend turn out?

BOBBI. Awful. Tom Wolfe was right. You can't go home again.

CHARLES. (*To Myra.*) Bobbi was home for a protest.

BOBBI. To Ingersoll.

MYRA. Where the cheese comes from?

BOBBI. You got it. And like they were crowning the Cheese Queen down at the arena, eh? The Cheese Queen! Like I mean gimmee a break. These sixteen year-olds get into bathing suits and wave like idiots on top of a hay wagon full of cheddar cheese. How come? So they can be Cheese Queen and get this tacky crown from the mayor who is, like, this old guy with hair growing out of his ears. Talk about sexist degradation.

CHARLES. So Bobbi quite rightly decided to protest.

BOBBI. Handed out pamphlets and everything.

CHARLES. And?

BOBBI. A bunch of jerky guys called me a 'lesbo gearbox.' But they were better than the mayor.

MYRA. What did he call you?

BOBBI. A 'silly wee girly.' Was I mad??? I jumped on the haywagon, grabbed the microphone and shouted, "I am not a silly wee girly, you patronizing wimp. My name is Bobbi Roy, I am an eighteen-year-old woman, and I'm on a town scholarship to Lakeview University."

CHARLES. I love it.

BOBBI. My folks didn't. They said they were ashamed of me. So I said, "If you're ashamed of me for standing up for human dignity then I'm ashamed of you!" Big mistake. I mean talk about blood on the linoleum. Yelling and screaming all night until Mom's crying, I'm crying, everybody's crying except my Dad who's hitting the refrigerator. It's hard being a feminist in Ingersoll.

CHARLES. They'll come around.

BOBBI. Not Dad. He's like an elephant in pants. He got me so mad I wrote these poems.

CHARLES. So it wasn't a total loss.

BOBBI. No. But boy, talk about suffering for your art.

CHARLES. I look forward to reading them.

(*MYRA, barely containing herself, begins loudly pressing the buttons of her tape recorder.*)

BOBBI. (*Awkwardly.*) Thanks, and, well, I guess I better go. See you later this week. (*To Myra.*) See you in class. (*To both.*) Sorry for interrupting. Bye.

CHARLES. Night.

(*CHARLES closes the door after her and turns with a happy smile. MYRA is eyeing him suspiciously. CHARLES stops smiling.*)

MYRA. (*Pause.*) "How did your weekend turn out?"

CHARLES. I like her.

MYRA. I thought you had standards.

CHARLES. She's got talent.

MYRA. Charles, I don't want to disillusion you but Bobbi Roy is not one of the sharpest tacks on the bulletin board. She can't even speak. She says "like I mean" until I want to "like I mean" strangle her.

CHARLES. All she needs is encouragement.

MYRA. She already suffers from hope. Encouraging it would be cruelty to a dumb animal.

CHARLES. Have you read her poems?

MYRA. Her essays are sufficient.

CHARLES. Then you have no right to judge.

MYRA. I have every right. Bobbi Roy is one book you *can* judge by its cover. She's a grab bag of causes; a library without a filing system. She is profoundly trivial.

(*CHARLES, who has glanced down at the poems in his hand, hands the top one to Myra.*)

MYRA. What am I supposed to do with this?

CHARLES. Surprise yourself.

MYRA. (*Reading skeptically.*)

"My skin is on fire
My hair flares skyward
My lungs explode
And
My throat rips open
With a scream of rage:
I will rot in this desert
No dreams to wash my bones."

And I always thought Ingersoll was pastoral.

CHARLES. "No dreams to wash my bones" is original; an arresting image. It's good.

MYRA. Emotional vomit.

CHARLES. Fresh, vital and unpretentious. Bobbi Roy doesn't hide behind footnotes.

MYRA. As opposed to me?

CHARLES. We weren't talking about you.

MYRA. I wasn't saying we were.

CHARLES. You were.

MYRA. I *wasn't*.

CHARLES. Weren't you?

MYRA. Was I?

CHARLES. Where were we?

MYRA. I believe we were discussing eating when in walked Margaret Atwood disguised as a Twinkie. You said she has talent, I tried not to gag, and it's been great fun ever since.

CHARLES. Myra –

MYRA. She comes by often?

CHARLES. My God, you're nosy.

MYRA. I'm not nosy. I'm amazed. No wonder you keep her a secret.

CHARLES. What?

MYRA. Come on, we're both grownups. I must say she has terrific timing. "I only have one relationship that matters to me. But it's a secret." And in she walks right on cue.

CHARLES. Look, I may be a writer but I'm not *that* contrived. Bobbi just drops off poems.

MYRA. Please. No guilt on my account.

CHARLES. If you must know, my secret love isn't even for a woman!

MYRA. (*Completely stunned.*) It's not for a woman?

CHARLES. No.

MYRA. Oh. (*Beat.*) So is it for a man or a relative?

CHARLES. It's for my typewriter.

MYRA. Your typewriter?

CHARLES. You bet. Writing. It's a sickness, but when it's happening I don't ever want to get better. I'm off in a land where all the unrelated scraps of time and event, all the meaningless odds and ends I waste my life with, have shape. Form. Substance. In my little world, life has order. Meaning. And I'm free. With my typewriter I can take on the world. Say exactly what I mean. Think. Feel. And when it's there, to edit. I love to edit. Ruthlessly. The feel of a red pencil in my hand slicing through a newly typed page. The crackle of one line hitting hard against another. All the flab cut out. Tight. Taut. Muscular. It's a rush. A physical rush. And when it's right – when I've got it and it's good – not to sleep for fear of missing an idea, a phrase, the placement of a comma, that could make it better yet. Because I demand the best. And so I work. And work. To make it look simple. To make it look easy. Some people are stupid enough to think it is. But when I'm with my typewriter and we're humming, I don't care. We're doing it and I don't have time to worry about them. I don't have time to worry about anything – not death, not time, not anything but our little world where everything has meaning and I am in control. It's so important that it go well. So important that ... So ... (*Turns away. HE is suddenly near tears.*)

MYRA. Charles?

CHARLES. (*His back to her, still overcome.*) I'm sorry.

MYRA. I don't understand.

CHARLES. I know.

MYRA. What is it?

CHARLES. Nothing. (*Pours himself a drink.*)

MYRA. You can talk to me, you know. I'm a friend. I want to be a friend. Is it about the book? (*Pause.*) Is it about *Papers*? (*Pause.*) Tell me!

CHARLES. There's nothing to tell!

MYRA. That's why you're in tears? Because of nothing? What do you think I am? Stupid? Honest to God you make me sick.

CHARLES. Like clockwork.

MYRA. You can knock off the suffering artist routine. Right now. I don't know what your problem is but it's not my fault. So don't take it out on me.

CHARLES. I'm sorry, I'm sorry.

MYRA. It's about *Papers*, isn't it.

(*CHARLES nods.*)

MYRA. Is it the opening? The ending? The structure? The tone?

CHARLES. It's the opening, the ending, the structure, the tone, the characters, the plot. Its ... (*Makes a motion with his hands and lowers his head. Pause.*)

MYRA. Could you show it to me?

(*CHARLES shakes his head.*)

MYRA. I'd like to help.

CHARLES. You can't.

MYRA. You'd be surprised.

CHARLES. I said you can't.

MYRA. I'm a pretty fair editor. Now where is it?

CHARLES. (*Pause.*) On the table.

MYRA. (*Goes to writing table.*) Where on the table?

CHARLES. In front of you.

MYRA. There's nothing here.

CHARLES. That's right.

MYRA. So where is it?

CHARLES. (*Beat.*) It isn't.

MYRA. What?

CHARLES. Two words. First word 'it.' Second word 'isn't.' It isn't! Got it?

MYRA. It isn't??

CHARLES. Very good.

MYRA. At all???

CHARLES. (*Shakes his head.*) For six years I have sat at that typewriter. I have stared at a blank sheet of paper. And it has stared back. I have sat and sat and stared and stared and nothing has happened. Nothing! Periodically, out of desperation, I have ripped it out and replaced it with another. And another. And another. And started again. And again. And again. Staring at this blank sheet of paper. And it staring back. I sit and I stare and I sit and I stare, listening to the radiator and the relentless tick tick ticking of the clock, while the hours turn to weeks turn to months turn to six years, my God, and me sitting in the dark staring at a goddamn piece of paper this is driving me out of my mind! And everyone asking. "What are you working on?" "How's it coming?" And me saying anything to shut them up. Anything to make the questions go away. But they don't. Every day they get louder. And how do I tell them my voices have left me? How do I tell myself that? That – my God – they may never come again. Writing is who I am. If I don't write, what am I? And I sit and I sit and I sit trying to forget the clock that tells me life is short, it's drifting away, it's slipping away like water, I can't hold it, and every day is another day gone and time is running out and I may never write again.

MYRA. And so you invented *Papers*.

CHARLES. (*Lifting sheaf of blank papers.*) *Papers*. The story of my life. I mean what is my life? It's a pile of crap, that's what it is. It's nothing. I don't have a home. I don't have a family. I don't have anyone. Just a pile of ... papers! (*Hurls them in the air; then with false cheer –*) Ah well. Drink?

MYRA. You drink too much.

CHARLES. It's the one thing I still know how to do. (*Goes to pour one.*)

MYRA. (*Sharply.*) You know there just might be a connection between your drinking and your block.

CHARLES. You know there just might be. But if there isn't what's my excuse?

MYRA. Charles, you make it hard for me to sympathize.

CHARLES. I don't want sympathy. I want a drink.

MYRA. It won't help.

CHARLES. Says who. If it weren't for drink there wouldn't be Irish literature.

MYRA. Charles –

CHARLES. Enough. If I want clichés I'll watch the soaps. I don't want the "Charles, you have so much talent" speech. I don't want the "Charles, it hurts me to see you like this" speech. I've heard them before and they're boring.

MYRA. Unlike drinking till you pass out.

CHARLES. Beats the hell out of listening to you sober.

MYRA. I could help you.

CHARLES. (*Sarcastic.*) Really.

MYRA. I know how to structure. I could organize you.

CHARLES. I'd be your experiment, would I?

MYRA. I'm trying to help.

CHARLES. Operative word 'trying.'

MYRA. You need routine. A schedule.

CHARLES. You're a very nice woman, Myra, but you don't have a clue.

MYRA. Is that so.

CHARLES. That's so. You're a critic. You can take it apart but you can't put it together.

MYRA. Don't patronize me.

CHARLES. Don't patronize *me*. It's not a question of saying, "It's been five pages since the last water image – time to toss in a symbol." If the words aren't there you can't force them.

MYRA. So what do you do? Coax them with a case of scotch? Pray for inspiration with your head down a toilet?

CHARLES. They're from the gut, Myra. The heart.

MYRA. They're also from the head. They can be analyzed. Patterns of images, symbols, shapes.

CHARLES. You don't know what writing's about.

MYRA. I've spent my life studying what it's about. I know.

CHARLES. You know nothing.

MYRA. (*Icy.*) If it weren't for critics like me, writers like you would be dead and forgotten.

CHARLES. That's the fantasy you guys have to keep your jobs alive.

MYRA. At least I'm still working.

CHARLES. You call *The Post-Modernist Dialectic* work?

MYRA. It's an important theory.

CHARLES. Pretentious bullshit. Who reads that crap?

MYRA. Certainly not lightweights like you.

CHARLES. You thought I was brilliant when I did my party piece, "Nuclear Artist: Secular Priest or Merchant of Dreams."

MYRA. You showed promise.

CHARLES. It's my sucker piece for snobs. I mocked you and you swallowed it.

MYRA. I'm sorry for giving you credit. You *are* a joke.

CHARLES. Get out.

MYRA. I didn't plan to stay. (*Goes to collect her coat.*) I haven't any patience for drunks. I haven't any patience for burn-outs who've forgotten how to think.

CHARLES. At least I haven't forgotten how to feel. I don't pretend the only thing that exists is my brain.

MYRA. No. You pretend you don't even have one.

CHARLES. You're an emotional dyslexic.

MYRA. And you're a coward.

CHARLES. Me?!?

MYRA. Yes, you. Big man with the big mouth. You know why you can't write? Because you're on the run. Scared to deal with your life. Afraid to face your critics, the world, yourself. Hiding in a bottle –

CHARLES. What about you – hiding behind a dead lover.

(*MYRA strikes him, letting out an involuntary cry.*)

CHARLES. I'm sorry.

MYRA. You *are* sorry. Sorry, pathetic –

CHARLES. Forgive me.

MYRA. You're not even fit for co-eds. Correction. Barely fit for Bobbi Roy. I bet you impress the hell out of her. Well go ahead. Impress the feeble-minded. You sure don't impress me.

(*MYRA storms out slamming door. CHARLES throws it open, calling out.*)

CHARLES. Who cares?!? (*Slams door shut and circles the room in a rage.*) Who the hell are you anyway? (*HE sees typewriter, freezes, and is suddenly struck with an idea.*) I don't need you. I don't need any of you. (*Goes to it, excited, and quickly inserts sheet of paper. HE types as HE speaks.*) *Papers.* He was a fake. A fraud. And he had met his nightmare. Dash dash. Myra ..."

(*Reconsiders and types with great glee –*) "Millie ... Fitzroy. She was compulsive, abrasive and ..."

(*CHARLES stops typing, stuck. HE picks up the desk statue of the Buddha and rubs its belly for luck. Suddenly HE stops, stares intensely into space and says, with some wonder –*)

CHARLES. He loved her.

***Fade to black.***

**END OF ACT ONE**

## ACT II

*Professor MOIRA FITZSIMMONS continues her address from her lectern.*

MOIRA. In Chapter Five we hit the scandal. You all know about the scandal. That's why you're here. To get more dirt. Well scandal aside, Martin Edwards and I parted friends. Anyone who says otherwise is a liar. And we behaved like adults. Except on the subject of co-eds. In my opinion, men don't deserve second childhoods until they're ninety. By then who cares. Edwards maintained that he was always a perfect gentleman when it came to young poets of the female persuasion. But he didn't fool me, nor a certain little tramp who shall remain nameless; but we all know who you are. I don't blame him. Memory plays tricks. So does fiction. As witness his treatment of Bobbi Roy. The 'complication.' (*Reads.*) "Most poets are like bugs. Best left under rocks. But Bobbi Roy was different. To her, being misunderstood wasn't an aesthetic principle: it was a way of life."

(*LIGHT out on MOIRA and up on Charles' front room ...*)

## ACT II

### Scene 1

*Early evening. CHARLES is on stage with BOBBI ROY. HE has poured them scotch. She has barely touched hers: too busy talking – earnest and very confused.*

BOBBI. You're the only one who understands. Not my folks. They want me to be a hairdresser. And when I tell them I want to be a poet they get weird. See they don't think poems are something you *write*. They don't even think poems are something you *read*. I mean the last poem they even *saw* was in a birthday card. It's so frustrating. I love them and I can't talk to them about something that means so much to me it makes me want to burst. And that hurts. I mean it really hurts, you know?

CHARLES. I know.

BOBBI. I know you know. Oh Mr. Martin, you've no idea how fantastic it is to talk to you. Like if I told this stuff to guys in my class they'd look real serious and nod their heads like they cared but all the time they'd be thinking, "How do I get into her pants." Real sensitive, eh? But you're beyond that. Like at your age you don't care about that stuff.

CHARLES. Just how old do you think I am?

BOBBI. I don't know. Older. Like my dad.

CHARLES. Right.

BOBBI. Do you mind getting older, Mr. Martin?

CHARLES. No. But I could do without the "Mister." Charles is fine.

BOBBI. I can't call you that.

CHARLES. Sure you can.

BOBBI. I *can't*. You're somebody. You're *it*. You're *there*. And I don't even know where I *am* let alone how to get where *you* are.

CHARLES. Don't try to get where I am.

BOBBI. But I have to. Like ever since I was little, like even before I could spell, I've had these overwhelming feelings I've just had to let out. They just keep coming at me and coming at me and coming at me until if I don't write them down I'm going to scream. They're who I am. They're what makes me different. Oh Mr. Martin, I want to be special. But everybody laughs at me. They hate me. They want me to fail.

CHARLES. They don't.

BOBBI. They do. But I'll show them. I'm going to be the best poet in the whole world. And I'm going to walk up the main street of Ingersoll and shout, "So there!"

CHARLES. Bravo!

BOBBI. Except that – oh Mr. Martin, I have a terrible secret and it's going to stop me from ever being a poet at all.

CHARLES. (*Very concerned.*) What?

BOBBI. I've been getting these awful headaches and they won't go away.

CHARLES. Are you sick?

BOBBI. Not really. I just want to die.

CHARLES. Have you seen a doctor?

BOBBI. There's nothing he can do. (*Very seriously.*) You see, it's my brain. Please don't tell anyone, because it's very private, but oh Mr. Martin I'm afraid I'm stupid.

CHARLES. You're not stupid.

BOBBI. I am. I can tell. In Ingersoll I could fake it. I mean you can know everything there is to know in Ingersoll and be a complete moron. But here – here there's not only books but people who read them. And I'm overcome with this terrible certainty that I'm dumb as a doorknob, simple as a dodo.

CHARLES. Don't be stupid.

BOBBI. Aaaa!

CHARLES. Sorry.

BOBBI. It's a nightmare. Life used to be simple. I knew everything. Like if I was going to be a poet I should study poetry. That's why I enrolled in Fitzpatrick's survey course. English 101: Abandon hope all ye who enter here.

CHARLES. Myra's good.

BOBBI. Oh yeah? She drones on and on reaming off secondary sources I've never heard of and I'm lost. Like I'm just sitting there staring at her. I feel like a frozen trout. At first I didn't care cuz it was only Chaucer. Old English, gimme a break: how do you understand that? It's a whole other language. And like they wrote it with sticks and feathers. I figured things would lighten up when we hit the Renaissance. But I didn't count on Spenser! He rhymes 'might', with 'plight' and 'smite' for ten thousand pages and I'm on the floor in a coma. And then there's Milton. Talk about Paradise Lost!

CHARLES. Maybe you should wait for the twentieth century.

BOBBI. That's what I thought. Until I encountered T.S. Eliot and started seriously thinking about group therapy.

CHARLES. I understand.

BOBBI. I wish I did. I sit for hours and hours reading the same words over and over and I don't get it.

CHARLES. You don't understand it?

BOBBI. I don't understand what's not to understand! I mean I get that Eliot thinks life is pretty depressing. So like is that profound or what am I missing? I don't know. I can't tell cuz half the time he doesn't write about what he's writing about. Like he's writing about cats; and I'm thinking, "Okay, he's writing about cats." Only he's not writing about cats; he's writing about the Egyptian Book of the Dead. And next thing you know he's not even writing in English. He's writing in Latin and Greek and Babylonian and I'm so confused I want to throw up.

CHARLES. It can't be that bad.

BOBBI. It's worse. Cuz I have to do an appreciation of Eliot for my major essay and it's already late and I haven't even started because I don't know where to start because – oh Mr. Martin I can't read ancient Babylonian! Help me! My life is a big, black pit and I'm falling and there's nothing to hold on to and what am I going to do? Why am I here? Who am I fooling? Why was I born?

CHARLES. It's only an essay.

BOBBI. (*Getting progressively faster.*) It's my life. If I fail I'll lose my term which means I'll lose my average which means I'll lose my scholarship which means I'll be back in Ingersoll where they laugh at me. I don't fit in. I'll never fit in. Anywhere. Ever. And I'll never be a poet either! My life is over!

CHARLES. It isn't.

BOBBI. But what if my folks are right? What if they're all right? What if I can't write? What if I just scribble? What if I'm a failure? What if I'm forgotten? What if – what if – what if – I might as well be dead but oh God Mr. Martin I don't want to die. I don't want to be stuck in a box. No. Not rotting in a black hole with worms crawling through my coffin. Maggots in my nose, ears and mouth. Trapped under the ground, all alone forever, under this heavy stone, all covered in weeds with no one to remember me and – oh God I can't stop it. Everywhere I turn is death. I look at babies and all I see are ninety year-olds in diapers. They gurgle and I hear death rattles. My life is this horrible roller coaster that's out of control and it scares me and makes me sick but when it stops it's all over and I'm gone and – oh Mr. Martin you've got to help me!

CHARLES. How?

BOBBI. Tell me I'm wrong!

CHARLES. You're wrong!

BOBBI. You're just saying that. Oh God, I can't think. I can't sleep. I just lie awake with this overwhelming fear that I'm gonna die and so what. And I'm numb and I'm sweating and I wish I was dead only that's what I'm scared of and and and – Ingersoll! Ingersoll!! I don't want to die in Ingersoll!!! I don't want to be stuck in that cemetery with all those dead farmers!!! I hate Fitzpatrick! I hate her!!! I'm going to die and it's all her fault!!! (*Bursts into tears.*)

CHARLES. (*Awkward pause while BOBBI cries.*) Please don't cry.

BOBBI. I'm not crying. I'm thinking.

CHARLES. (*Kindly.*) Well, while you're thinking do you want a Kleenex?

BOBBI. I want to die.

(*Pause. CHARLES flaps his arms helplessly, not knowing what to do, as BOBBI continues to whimper into her hands.*)

CHARLES. Uh, Bobbi, you should talk to someone.

BOBBI. That's why I'm here.

CHARLES. But you need a grownup. Not me. I'm this, this – well look at me. I'm just an eight year-old in disguise.

BOBBI. You're the only one who cares about me.

CHARLES. Hey.

BOBBI. I mean it. I don't have any friends. Just people I spend time with.

CHARLES. (*Pause.*) Okay. Let's talk. (*Short pause as he organizes his thoughts.*) Your problem is you're going to die and be forgotten.

BOBBI. (*Small voice.*) I don't want to die. I don't want to be forgotten.

CHARLES. Right. I got that. You made that clear. But you're afraid you're going to die and be forgotten. Why? Because you'll be in Ingersoll ...

(*BOBBI sobs.*)

CHARLES. ... because you'll lose your scholarship because you'll lose your average because you'll fail this essay. Is that right?

BOBBI. (*Small voice.*) Un-huh.

CHARLES. So, as I see it, your problem is this essay. Right?

BOBBI. And I haven't even started.

CHARLES. We'll solve that right now. First sentence. "T.S. Eliot is a major poet of the twentieth century." There now. You've started.

BOBBI. Then what?

CHARLES. Why don't I get my copy of Eliot and we'll work on it.

BOBBI. You'll help me?

CHARLES. Absolutely.

BOBBI. You've saved my life.

CHARLES. No problem. I suspect you probably know a lot more about Eliot than you think.

BOBBI. Really?

CHARLES. Absolutely. You're just having a block.

BOBBI. Just a block? You don't know what it's like.

CHARLES. When it comes to blocks I'm a pro. I'm blocked all the time. In fact I was once blocked for six years.

BOBBI. I'd shoot myself!

CHARLES. Thanks. I'll keep it in mind for next time.

BOBBI. How did you get unblocked?

CHARLES. I came here, met people and got ideas.

BOBBI. About what?

CHARLES. Writers and academics.

BOBBI. You mean like Fitzpatrick?

CHARLES. (*Smiles.*) Not exactly.

BOBBI. Oh my God! You're writing about Fitzpatrick!!! What's it called?

CHARLES. *Papers*, and that's a secret.

BOBBI. Am I in it?

CHARLES. Let's talk about Eliot.

BOBBI. I'm in a book by Charles Martin!!!

CHARLES. The universal in Eliot.

BOBBI. Am I a sympathetic character?

(*There is a KNOCK on the front door.*)

BOBBI. Should I come back later?

CHARLES. (*Going to door.*) No. Stay there.

BOBBI. Wait. I'm a mess. Let me wash my face.

CHARLES. You know where it is?

BOBBI. Uh-huh. (*About to exit down corridor to washroom.*) You know, I wish I was your age. I just feel so young. (*Exits down corridor.*)

CHARLES. I just feel so old. (*Answers the front door. Myra is standing outside, carrying a large briefcase. Surprised to see her.*) Myra!

MYRA. (*Not knowing what to say.*) Charles!

CHARLES. Yes, well, what can I do for you?

MYRA. Yes, well, may I come in?

CHARLES. (*Uncertain.*) Uh – certainly, yes.

MYRA. I won't keep you because I'm sure you're very busy – I'm busy myself – up to my ears in term papers – they go on forever – but I just finished a draft of the book – "Charles Martin And The Etcetera?"

CHARLES. Yes?

MYRA. Yes and, well, I was in the neighbourhood so I thought, well, I have it here with me. I thought you might like to have a look. (*Indicates briefcase.*)

CHARLES. There's no rush is there?

MYRA. Oh no. I was just out walking and I happened to have it with me. (*Retrieves it from her briefcase.*)

CHARLES. Thank you.

MYRA. No, no. Thank *you*. Your help was so appreciated.

CHARLES. Any time.

MYRA. (*Awkward beat, hesitant smile.*) Thanks. And, well there are a few details I don't have quite right. I was wondering if maybe you might go over them with me?

CHARLES. Now?

MYRA. Not if it's inconvenient.

CHARLES. It is a bit late.

MYRA. Of course. Well I won't keep you then. Except to say – except to say I lied.

CHARLES. Pardon?

MYRA. I didn't come because of the book.

CHARLES. You didn't?

MYRA. I know this is foolish but I was up in my room staring out my window, nursing a sherry – stacks of 101 papers on all sides – and suddenly I felt cold and I already had on two sweaters and suddenly I couldn't be there. I had to be out. And – well I had the book and I know I should have phoned first but, well, I would have felt so silly because what would I have said? "Hello Charles, I already have on two sweaters but I'm still cold, I can't be here, I have to be out and I have my book?" I mean, really, can you imagine?

So anyway I didn't and I'm here and I'm sorry. I shouldn't have come. I'm sorry.

CHARLES. Don't be.

MYRA. It's just that I felt so lonely. How embarrassing.

CHARLES. Not at all.

MYRA. And I had to be with someone. I couldn't just sit there alone with my term papers, staring out the window at all these people passing by – all of them smiling and all of them with someone – they were so happy I wanted to hit them! I felt I was suffocating. And then I thought of you and those wonderful times we had together reading, talking, just being together and, well I had to see you. I had to tell you how very very sorry I am about those things I said. I want to take them back. I wish I could cut out my tongue. I didn't mean it. I really didn't. Especially what I said about drinking and co-eds.

(*Unseen by Myra, CHARLES casts a guilty look down the corridor.*)

MYRA. It was unfair and cheap and I'm sorry.

CHARLES. I'm sorry for what I said too. Especially about your fiancé.

MYRA. Thank you. Thank you and – oh Charles it's so good to talk to you again, to be with you. I shouldn't be so personal, it isn't at all like me, but as I sat in my room I thought to myself,

"Myra, Charles was right. You spend your whole life thinking. When are you going to feel? When are you going to act?" And I thought, "tonight. I'm taking the plunge tonight. For once I'm not going to hide behind ideas. For once I'm just going to be me." My Lord it was terrifying coming here and knocking on your door. But now that I'm here and saying what's been locked up inside I feel – well I feel such a release. It's so very strange. But so very wonderful. Because you understand, I know you do. You're lonely too, you understand what it means, what it does, we're so very alike and –

(*BOBBI appears at the doorway to interior. THEY freeze.*)

BOBBI. Hi.

MYRA. (*To Charles.*) I seem to have come at a bad time.

CHARLES. No, no.

BOBBI. (*Heading to her drink on coffee table.*) I'll just get my drink and get out of your hair. (*To Myra.*) Sorry I still haven't finished my paper. But it's coming along real well. It's going to have lots of original insights.

MYRA. What a treat.

CHARLES. At the moment we're working our way through "The Love Song of J. Alfred Prufrock."

MYRA. So I see.

BOBBI. (*Solemnly.*) T.S. Eliot is very profound.

MYRA. You don't say.

BOBBI. Yeah. Well anyway, I think I'll disappear. (*Picking up her drink.*) It sure is exciting being in a book, isn't it?

MYRA. Pardon?

BOBBI. *Papers.*

MYRA. (*To Charles.*) So you've been working.

BOBBI. And to think it's all about us!

MYRA. Fancy that. (*To Charles, tight smile.*) How does it turn out?

CHARLES. (*Awkward.*) I'm not sure.

MYRA. Keep me posted.

BOBBI. (*To Charles.*) I'll be back there when you're ready. (*To Myra.*) Nice talking to you.

MYRA. And so nice talking to you.

BOBBI. (*Little wave salute.*) See ya.

MYRA. (*Little wave salute.*) See ya.

(*BOBBI exits down corridor with her drink.*)

MYRA. And I suppose I'll see you too. Sorry to have intruded.

CHARLES. Myra, wait.

MYRA. For what? You are deep in 'literary' pursuits and I am clearly in the way. But don't worry about me. A good brisk walk will solve everything. It always does.

CHARLES. I'm sorry.

MYRA. Nothing to be sorry about. Myra's just in one of her moods. You see, I didn't really need to see you. I just thought if you hadn't anything else to do, but you do, so maybe next time if I'm free.

CHARLES. If you'd like to stay –

MYRA. An evening with Miss Roy is not on my agenda. I should get back anyway. I'm expecting a number of very important phone calls. You should be ashamed.

CHARLES. It's not what you think.

MYRA. I'm not blind.

CHARLES. If I can explain. Just a few words–

MYRA. I don't need your words. I have enough of my own. My whole life is words. Words words words!!! I am sick to goddamn death of words. I want to scream. I am in pain and all I can think are sentences! I wish to God I were illiterate!

CHARLES. (*Comforting.*) It's all right.

MYRA. (*Shaking him off.*) It is not all right. It is pain and it is anger and it is humiliation and I cannot stand it any more. I cannot! You know, just because I have a brain doesn't mean I don't have a heart!

CHARLES. What?

MYRA. You have hurt me. You have ... have ... I cannot breathe you have hurt me.

CHARLES. What did I do?

MYRA. You used me, dammit! You used me!!!

CHARLES. What?

MYRA. I came here to tell you I love you and I find I'm a plot twist!!!

CHARLES. You love me?

MYRA. Put it in Chapter Five. Big laugh!

CHARLES. I'm not laughing.

MYRA. Why not? I'm comic relief. All I can do is mark papers and read. Ask the Dean. I can't even attract flies.

CHARLES. That's not true.

MYRA. Terrific. I *can* attract flies. What else have you put in your book?

CHARLES. Nothing. Nothing.

MYRA. Don't give me that.

CHARLES. Uh, just Robert, your fiancé, I, uh–

MYRA. That's in your book too?

CHARLES. It's tragic.

MYRA. Oh God you didn't. Oh God you couldn't.

CHARLES. I changed the names

MYRA. For everyone to read? To know? To gossip?? (*Hyperventilating and crying.*) I seem to be losing control. (*Wipes her eyes briskly.*) Thank God I don't wear makeup.

CHARLES. (*Reaches out to her.*) Myra, please understand –

MYRA. GET AWAY FROM ME! T.S. Eliot was right!

CHARLES. Pardon?

MYRA. "Between the Idea and the Reality/Falls the Shadow"!!!

(*MYRA runs out into the night leaving a bewildered Charles alone on stage.*)

**BLACKOUT**

## ACT TWO

### Scene 2

*Myra's office; a cosy wall of books. Perhaps a tea kettle and coffee makings. MYRA is seated behind her desk, glasses on, taking notes from a very serious book. And loving it. BOBBI appears at the doorway. SHE knocks hesitantly.*

MYRA. Yes?

BOBBI. (*Short pause.*) Uh ... hi. Sorry I haven't been to class.

MYRA. We've coped.

BOBBI. (*Awkward beat.*) May I come in?

MYRA. I suppose.

BOBBI. (*Enters.*) This sure is a nice office. I mean I just love those books! They make this place look like one of those family rooms in "Better Homes and Gardens."

MYRA. (*Very dry.*) I've always maintained books are a safe way to do a wall if you can't pick art.

BOBBI. So, like, have you actually read the whole wall?

MYRA. Of course.

BOBBI. That's pretty serious reading.

MYRA. They're pretty serious books.

BOBBI. I'd go blind.

MYRA. You might. But now, if you don't mind, I'm in the middle of a major discovery, so let's cut the small talk, shall we? What do you want?

BOBBI. My Eliot essay.

MYRA. Ah yes. (*Glances through her 'Out" tray.*) You were gone so long I'd almost forgotten about it. (*Gives it to her.*)

BOBBI. Thanks.

MYRA. Don't mention it.

BOBBI. (*Seeing mark.*) F?

MYRA. F.

BOBBI. So what's that supposed to mean?

MYRA. (*Sweet, patient smile.*) You fail.

BOBBI. That's not fair.

MYRA. Welcome to life.

BOBBI. You didn't give this essay any thought.

MYRA. Neither did you.

BOBBI. I did too. It says exactly what I think.

MYRA. How frightening.

BOBBI. And it's good – it really is – and you gotta pass me. If you don't I'll die! I'll just die!!

MYRA. Miss Roy, it's too early in the day for the last act of *Camille.*

BOBBI. But you don't understand. Without a pass my scholarship is doomed!

MYRA. That's a shame. But hardly relevant.

BOBBI. Yeah. The only thing that's relevant is you wanted to fail me so you failed me.

MYRA. There are good, solid reasons to fail that essay.

BOBBI. Name one.

MYRA. I'll name you a dozen. Give it here. (*Takes essay.*) Let's start with the title: "Ingersoll and the Objective Corelative." Two 'R's in 'correlative.' You should invest in a dictionary.

BOBBI. What for? I mean why look up words you think you spell right?

MYRA. Don't be smart.

BOBBI. I'm just stating an opinion.

MYRA. You don't have opinions. You have notions. Such as: (*Reading from Bobbi's essay with vague distaste.*) "One can't read T.S. Eliot. One has to decode him. He's the original game of Trivial Pursuit. And that's not art. It's pretension." (*To Bobbi.*) And that's not an essay. It's a diatribe.

BOBBI. But it's true. He's a tight-ass.

MYRA. He's profound.

BOBBI. He sucks. "This is the way the world ends/Not with a bang but a whimper." You call that deep? It's just the same old song and dance about how the world is a sterile dust heap and everything's pointless so why not just die because what does it matter anyway. Like I mean I just want to say, 'Lighten up, eh?'

MYRA. "LIGHTEN UP"?

BOBBI. Sure. He acts like it's the world's fault he's a boring old prude with a bad sex life.

MYRA. You offend me. Deeply. To trash the most important force in modern poetry without so much as a footnote!

BOBBI. You mean if I quoted academics you wouldn't mind.

MYRA. Those who have devoted their lives to literature deserve serious attention. Not some teenager who can't even spell.

BOBBI. Well somebody who's devoted his life to literature takes me very seriously.

MYRA. Who?

BOBBI. Mr. Martin.

MYRA. Mister. Aren't we formal.

BOBBI. He likes my instincts.

MYRA. I'm sure he does.

BOBBI. And he liked this essay.

MYRA. He can like what he wants. He doesn't teach this class.

BOBBI. So what? He knows books. And those are his ideas.

MYRA. They are?

BOBBI. Yeah.

MYRA. Then you get zero. For plagiarism.

BOBBI. You're just jealous!

MYRA. *What?*

BOBBI. Lonely and jealous! Well I'm sorry! But it's not my fault you love Mr. Martin!

MYRA. (*Stunned.*) That is the most bizarre collection of sentences I've heard in my life!

BOBBI. It's the truth and you know it.

MYRA. What I know is that you have a gift for fantasy.

BOBBI. Be smug as you like. I was in the hall. I heard all about you and Mr. Martin and your lover.

MYRA. You filthy little sneak!

BOBBI. I didn't mean to. But it got so interesting.

MYRA. My conversations are private!

BOBBI. And that's how I was going to leave them. Until this.

MYRA. What do you mean 'until this'?

BOBBI. Well it's pretty obvious.

MYRA. Are you suggesting I failed you for personal reasons?

BOBBI. You got it.

MYRA. I am a professional. I don't descend to personalities, no matter how distasteful.

BOBBI. Bullshit.

MYRA. Don't bullshit me, young lady.

BOBBI. Then don't bullshit me. You're no more objective than that prissy old T.S. Eliot. You just have a lot of fancy words to cover up how mean and nasty you really are.

MYRA. Get out of my office.

BOBBI. Don't worry. I'm going. I'm going straight to the Dean.

MYRA. I beg your pardon?

BOBBI. If you don't pass this essay, your life will be hell.

MYRA. Are you threatening me?

BOBBI. Standing up for my rights.

MYRA. Three cheers for 'Bimbo Liberation.'

BOBBI. Very funny. Let's see if the Dean laughs when he hears about your ethics. (*Runs out.*)

MYRA. (*Calling after her.*) Ethics! Ethics!!! (*To self.*) That's rich. Blackmailed by a little bitch who talks about ethics!

**BLACKOUT**

## ACT II

### Scene 3

*CHARLES is alone onstage in Myra's office. HE is holding the manuscript Myra left him in Act II, Scene 1. HE looks around, then places the manuscript on her desk. HE considers leaving but instead moves behind her desk and sits. Pause while HE looks at the walls, waiting. Enter BOBBI in a rush. SHE stops suddenly, surprised and a little embarrassed to see him.*

BOBBI. Uh – hi.

CHARLES. Hi.

BOBBI. I was expecting Professor Fitzpatrick.

CHARLES. So was I.

BOBBI. She told me to be here at two and – oh Mr. Martin, I'm sorry. I want to be buried in sand and forgotten. I want to be spread out on a tarmac and have an airplane run over my head. I want –

CHARLES. What are you talking about?

BOBBI. The Dean. I saw the Dean. Boy did I see the Dean. I tried to stay normal but he just smoked his pipe, like I was wasting his time. And the more he smoked the madder I got until suddenly I'm waving my arms and roaring.

CHARLES. Slow down. You're at the Dean's and you're upset?

BOBBI. Upset? I'm like the Valkyries on acid. And I hear these words coming out of my mouth. About you and me and Professor Fitzpatrick. Don't hate me.

CHARLES. I don't.

BOBBI. Well *I* do. And so does the Dean. He went on and on about ethics and honour until I couldn't think. It was awful. Like being smothered in porridge.

CHARLES. What did you say?

BOBBI. That she failed me because she was jealous.

CHARLES. What???

BOBBI. You didn't know? I thought you were here to lecture me.

CHARLES. I'm here to return a manuscript.

BOBBI. Oh no! You didn't know and I told you and it's the end of the year and I'll never see you again and you'll remember me as this stupid little twit with a big mouth and it's all my fault! Oh God, I want to be covered in garbage and eaten by rats! I want –

(*Enter MYRA with coffee cup. SHE is surprised to see the two of them there together.*)

MYRA. (*To Charles.*) Why Mr. Martin, what a surprise. (*To Bobbi.*) Reinforcements?

CHARLES. I came to return your manuscript. I'll drop by later.

MYRA. You can stay. What I have to say to Miss Roy would get back to you anyway. (*To Bobbi.*) I was speaking to the Dean. I understand you're quite the little orator.

BOBBI. I'm sorry. I'm really, really sorry.

MYRA. In his opinion the matter is closed. Your essay fails as marked.

BOBBI. (*About to cry.*) Can I go now?

MYRA. No. Because as far as *I* am concerned the matter is *not* closed. There have been serious charges of impropriety.

BOBBI. I already said I was sorry.

MYRA. I don't care what you said. This isn't a conversation; it's a monologue. I talk. You listen. Your essay was, is, and will remain, a failure. (*Short pause.*) However, justice must not only be done but be *seen* to be done. Therefore, to avoid any implication of personal bias, I will not include that failure when averaging your final mark.

BOBBI. What?

MYRA. I believe that will leave you enough to keep your scholarship.

BOBBI. (*Bewildered, overcome with joy.*) I can't believe it.

MYRA. As I have been at pains to point out, what you believe and what is the truth are not necessarily the same thing.

BOBBI. Thank you. I mean – like I mean thank you!

(*BOBBI embraces Myra, who doesn't know quite how to react.*)

MYRA. There's nothing to thank me for. Your apology is, by the way, accepted.

BOBBI. I don't know what to say.

MYRA. Have a nice summer.

BOBBI. Have a nice summer.

MYRA. You too.

BOBBI. (*To Charles.*) Will I see you before you leave?

CHARLES. You bet.

BOBBI. Great. I gotta tell you all about my summer job. The Ingersoll Times wants me to write a weekly column.

CHARLES. A published author!

BOBBI. Yeah. And all on account of the stink I made about the Cheese Queen. Like they think I'm this big, local radical, eh? Cracks me up.

CHARLES. Good luck.

BOBBI. Thanks. (*To Myra.*) Now I got this image I guess I better "prepare a face to meet the faces that I meet."

MYRA. Prufrock.

BOBBI. Yeah. Anyway, see you later.

CHARLES. You too.

BOBBI. (*To Myra.*) Thanks again. Bye! (*Runs out, full of energy.*)

MYRA. Now then, you have a manuscript for me?

CHARLES. (*Points to desk.*) Yours. It's very good.

MYRA. Thank you.

CHARLES. No. Thank *you*. You really captured my work.

MYRA. That's my job. (*Short pause, hesitant.*) You're all packed?

CHARLES. Pretty much.

MYRA. When do you leave?

CHARLES. End of the week.

MYRA. I never get used to it. The end of term. Time. It goes so quickly. It seems just yesterday you were arriving and suddenly it's spring and you're gone. Soon everyone will be gone. The campus will be deserted. (*Pause.*) It's been nice knowing you. I'm glad you dropped in.

CHARLES. Did you think I'd leave without saying goodbye?

MYRA. I try not to expect things.

CHARLES. I've tried calling. A lot actually. You haven't been in.

MYRA. No. I've been busy.

CHARLES. I've missed you.

MYRA. The library. When times are ... awkward ... I virtually move in.

CHARLES. I said I missed you.

MYRA. I know. They really ought to give me a pillow with my stack pass.

CHARLES. About Bobbi ...

MYRA. I don't want to talk about it. I really don't.

CHARLES. There's a misunderstanding.

MYRA. I don't think so.

CHARLES. She's a student.

MYRA. Don't remind me.

CHARLES. That's *all* she is.

MYRA. I see the two of you alone. At your house. At night. I see you both around. For God's sake, I can't even walk into my own office without seeing you together.

CHARLES. To paraphrase a remarkable woman, "The truth and what you think is the truth are not necessarily the same things."

MYRA. Please. I don't feel well.

CHARLES. You do this to yourself, you know.

MYRA. I know what I know what I know what I know. And I know that I don't want to discuss this any more. I feel it starting. In the stomach. This sick, empty sense of nothing. And it surges through you – your fingers, your chest, your head – until you're sea-sick. Numb, nauseous, unable to breathe.

CHARLES. You make me want to shake you.

MYRA. She's a lovely girl, Charles. Unfinished, untutored and unformed. But she has a future. And it's fresh and full of promise. It's awfully hard not to hate someone like that. To see it. And not be able to have it. I'm happy for her. I'm happy for you. Now please, leave me alone.

CHARLES. No!

MYRA. Charles, there is a thick glass wall between me and the world. It's a lovely view but there aren't any doors. I don't want to think about it. I can't. I won't be pathetic. Please.

CHARLES. Do you know the last time I heard you say something nice about yourself? Do you? It was never.

MYRA. That's not true.

CHARLES. Your mind is on overdrive running yourself into the ground. Over and over and over. You're relentless. Dumping on yourself, hurting yourself, destroying yourself. My God I admire your stamina but it terrifies me.

MYRA. You don't know what you're talking about.

CHARLES. I don't know neurotics? You're telling me *I* don't know *neurotics?*

MYRA. So now I'm neurotic.

CHARLES. Your problem isn't that people don't love you. Your problem is you won't let them.

MYRA. There is no problem. Because I don't care.

CHARLES. You cared about Robert.

MYRA. Don't.

CHARLES. You loved him and he loved you.

MYRA. Please don't!

CHARLES. And you have standards. You don't accept second rate. So he must have been terrific.

MYRA. He was nothing!

CHARLES. Nothing? You live for his memory!!

MYRA. I live for nothing! Nothing, dammit!! Nothing!!!

CHARLES. Wake up!

MYRA. No, you wake up! Robert didn't die! We weren't going to be married!! He – Charles, he doesn't exist!! (*Pause, then slow and quiet.*) I'm sorry. We were talking. About my life. About my work *being* my life. And it hurt me. So deeply. There has never been anyone. And I felt so alone. And I felt so strange. And peculiar. And ... I found myself wanting so much. Just for there to have been someone. *Someone.* And I heard myself saying this lie. This terrible lie. Forgive me. I just wanted to feel wanted. To feel normal. I'm so sorry. I just didn't want to be alone.

(*There is a long, painful silence. Slowly, awkwardly, MYRA makes her way behind her desk, perhaps brushing her eyes with her hand. SHE sees her manuscript.*)

MYRA. (*Very quietly.*) I'm glad you like the book. I tried to do you justice.

CHARLES. Myra ...

MYRA. It's okay.

CHARLES. No. I hurt you.

MYRA. The truth never hurt anyone. (*Awkward smile.*) The trouble is you're right. I don't know how to feel. And I feel like a fool when I try.

CHARLES. But you do feel. And you're accurate. Your book ... I've never been able to connect. Not talking ... in person ... with people. But I always hoped if I worked hard enough I could reach them through words. I never felt I had. Until now. You know, Myra, the world would be a lot less lonely if we could only know for certain what just one other person was really thinking. We can't. But you and me: we make pretty good guesses. I don't know what else to say. You've seen through me. You know me. And you love me despite that. I didn't come here to say thank you, Myra. I came to say ... I love you too.

*(Pause. Slowly MYRA rises. They move towards each other hesitantly, then open their arms simultaneously and embrace, holding each other as the LIGHTS fade to black.*

*LIGHTS rise on Professor MOIRA FITZPATRICK behind her lectern.)*

MOIRA. "I love you." "I love you." The three hardest words in the language. I don't know if anyone ever heard Martin Edwards say those words. I don't know if it was possible for him to say them. But I do know he thought them. He gave them to his namesake in *Papers* – his most personal book. He gave them to Martin. Charles Martin. I love you. Martin Edwards chose those words to end his book. His last. And when I read those words, whatever awkwardness, whatever resentment, whatever pain I have felt is forgotten. As for anger – recent events have made that impossible. His readers, his friends, and especially all of us here at the university I'm sure, were shocked to hear of his sudden passing. Driving here to the cottage where he had planned to spend his summers ... The accident has been difficult to accept. But our lives are not books. We get what we get and not what we deserve. So we make do with memories and hope they're happy ones. Mine are.

(*LIGHTS fade on Moira and rise on the AUTHOR, who looks exactly like Charles. HE is alone, sitting in his living room, reading aloud from the last of a large loose leaf manuscript. Within seconds, it is clear that everything we have seen, including Professor Moira Fitzsimmons, has been part of his manuscript.*)

AUTHOR. (*Reading aloud.*) "Professor Moira Fitzsimmons concluded her address on Martin Edwards' novel, *Papers*. She discussed its form, structure, and the polarities of art/life, intellect/emotion, reality and illusion. Her lecture over, she returned to her office and sat, alone, staring out her window at the trees silhouetted against the lake. Outside the wind blew clouds against a bright moon. There would be a storm. But as Moira re-read Martin's final chapter, her mind, unlike the night, was calm. The End." (*AUTHOR turns over the last page, looks up and calls out.*) Well what do you think?

(*Enter ACADEMIC from hall with a tray of sandwiches. SHE looks exactly like Myra/Moira.*)

ACADEMIC. I'm glad you took my advice on my scene with that student. Absolutely accurate. But I'm still a bit uncomfortable.

AUTHOR. Worried about the gossip?

ACADEMIC. Living with you I've gotten used to it. No. It's the framing device. I wouldn't give a lecture like that even if you *were* dead. Speaking of which, that death has got to go.

AUTHOR. But think of the romance. The tragedy.

ACADEMIC. It's 'accident ex machina.'

AUTHOR. Are you kidding? It's the dialectical synthesis. Emotion lives through intellect. And Myra's fantasy of a dead lover becomes Moira's reality.

ACADEMIC. Please. You sound like me on a bad day.

AUTHOR. I'm tired of being called superficial.

ACADEMIC. You'd rather be fashionably bleak? Contrary to popular opinion there is nothing profound about despair. And there's nothing wrong with a happy ending. Especially if it's mine.

AUTHOR. But this is fiction.

ACADEMIC. Who else has published a book called *The Post-Modernist Dialectic?* It's us. Except that Charles is a sweetheart.

AUTHOR. I'm not?

ACADEMIC. You're fine. I just mean Charles actually tells Myra he loves her.

AUTHOR. I haven't told you?

ACADEMIC. No.

AUTHOR. Well I do.

ACADEMIC. What?

AUTHOR. You know.

ACADEMIC. Of course I know. But you still haven't said it.

AUTHOR.It's not what people say. At least not when they mean it.

ACADEMIC. So don't. (*Goes to leave.*)

AUTHOR. Myrna, I really do, you know. You're wonderful, fantastic, and I – I – I just don't know how to get the quotation marks off it.

ACADEMIC. You're such a twit.

AUTHOR. (*Opens his arms.*) I know.

(*ACADEMIC goes to him. THEY hug.*)

ACADEMIC. (*Kissing him.*) A twit. A nit. Why do you make me so mad?

AUTHOR. Because I love you, dammit.

ACADEMIC. (*Big grin, tight squeeze.*) And how I love you!

AUTHOR. And they lived, as far as possible, happily ever after.

(*THEY kiss as the LIGHTS fade to black.*)

**THE END**

## A Few Notes On *Papers*

I have enormous respect and admiration for most directors, actors and technicians. Driven by a commitment to quality, they are open to any suggestion that will improve the work.

By contrast, those few with the motto "No notes: a play should stand on its own" are the very sort who specialize in literary kneecapping. Having butchered one's work beyond recognition, they invite the corpse to rise from the dead and speak for itself. Whether they perceive a threat to their infallibility or honestly believe a play arranges itself by happy accident, they consider a playwright's suggestions especially irrelevant.

They may be right. Companies with insight and intelligence have generally foreseen one's concerns and taken them into account; whereas the very idiots who ought to have those concerns tattooed on their brains have tossed them in the garbage on principle.

But being a happy simpleton who enjoys hitting his head with a hammer, I've scribbled a few notes anyway. So to all of you for whom these thoughts go without saying, my deep thanks not only for giving my characters physical life but also for bearing with me as I state the obvious. To the rest, who have taught me that even foolproof scripts are no match for 'creative interpretation', a plea: These notes are intended to head off disaster. Please consider them an aid, not a challenge.

*Papers* is easy to misplay. It is poised between comedy and drama. To lean on one at the expense of the other is to undermine both.

It is also deceptive, not only in structure but in style. It appears to be realistic. But the characters are far more literate than people in everyday life. They revel in language. The right word is always on the tip of their tongues. They don't have to grope for it.

This verbal fluency is not only at the root of their sparring, it is part of their natures. Use it. If you toss in extra 'uhs' 'wells' and grunts, what should sparkle will collapse about your ears like a ten ton weight.

I should also note that I take as much care with punctuation as I do with words. Periods and commas are to text what rests are to music. They shape the phrasing and colour the content. As a rule, my characters and I place the meat of our comments at the end of our sentences. To break a line in the middle destroys not only its intent but its comic shape as well.

This verbal precision is *not* to suggest that the characters are joke machines. Their humour comes from character in situation and I respect them very much; none more so than Bobbi, the most easily misunderstood.

Bobbi is young. She is naive. She is scattered. But she is *not* stupid. Her fears about being inadequate, insignificant, and dead, are very real and should be treated seriously. Her reaction to those fears may be hysteria, but that's a function of age, not intelligence. If you play Bobbi as an airhead, her threat to Myra will be undermined, as will our respect for Charles.

That having been said, don't make the equally serious mistake of breast-beating these people into the ground. Self-pity is not only unattractive; it's counter-productive. My characters may be in pain. But, fortunately, they're bright. And in the case of Myra and Charles, they use wit, irony and a high degree of self-awareness to distance themselves from their emotions.

While this distancing contributes to their problems, it's also what gives them dignity: they bleed but they persevere. Only in rare moments do they come apart. (Charles, facing his block in Act One, Scene Two; Myra on the subject of her 'lover'). When that happens the effect is devastating – but only if we have previously seen them in control.

For instance, Charles' first speech about writing ("It's a sickness, but when it's happening I don't ever want to get better") should not be informed with the angst of his block. If it is, his 'blocked' speech, which follows, will be undercut and turn into a never-ending whine.

Charles' writing speech, in fact, should be exuberant, charged with excitement and joy. It's a speech he never intends to make. Quite simply, he's teasing Myra about his personal life when suddenly he finds himself talking about his great love and obsession.

The imagery in the speech is physical, sexual, and we should see his thrill in full bloom. It catches him off guard. And it is that sudden remembrance and recognition of how wonderful it is to write that causes his breakdown; and without which we cannot fully understand his pain and loss.

Speaking further of control, you'll get off to a good start if Myra takes charge on her first entrance. When she walks through the front door the world is her oyster. She's fought for Charles, she's got him, and through his books she knows him inside out – she thinks. The more Myra is in command, the more Charles will feel trapped: and the greater will be the tension and conflict which propels the comedy of Act One, Scene One.

This forthrightness is central to Myra. She is no shrinking violet. It is her directness and unwitting abrasiveness that have frightened off potential love interests, not a lack of attractiveness. Which is is a nice way of saying, don't make the mistake of turning Myra into a dowdy frump. She may not be a fashion plate, but she is very crisply turned out. Remember: being both single and a well-paid professional, she has a large disposable income. Her problem is that she grew up before it was polite for women to fight for their opinions.

This brings me to the question of the characters' ages. Although it is possible for Charles and Myra to be played late thirties, late forties or slightly older is best. The more mature these characters are, the greater their stakes become. Less time means less freedom to maneuver. They aren't just defending a few correctable choices. They're defending their lives. (Myra's virginity also makes more sense in a person born before the sexual revolution.)

But that having been said, what is *most* important is that you cast a Charles and Myra who can function as a couple. Without chemistry between your actors you're dead in the water. If you have to make a trade-off between late thirties actors who spark each other and older actors who don't, go with youth.

Ah well, enough said. These people are my friends. Be good to them and they will be good to you. Abuse them and may your every theatre nightmare come true.

All the best,
Have fun,

Allan Stratton

## COSTUME PLOT

CHARLES

I.1: light cord trousers, check shirt, socks, hush puppies, tie, sports jacket, wristwatch, glasses in case

Lose: tie, jacket, shoes

Add: pullover sweater, slippers

I.2: light cord trousers, check shirt, slippers, pullover sweater, socks

Interval

II.1: dark cords, plaid shirt, sneakers, socks, heavier sweater

Lose: sweater, sneakers

Add: turtleneck T-shirt, hush puppies, outdoor jacket (roll up shirt sleeves)

II.3: dark cords, plaid shirt, sleeves rolled up, turtleneck T-shirt, outdoor jacket, hush puppies, socks

Lose: outdoor jacket

Conclusion: dark cords, plaid shirt, sleeves rolled up, hush puppies, socks, turtleneck T-shirt

MYRA

Introduction: grey/blue suit, blouse with bow, blue court shoes, academic gown

Lose: academic

Add: cloth coat, handbag

I.1: grey/blue suit, blouse with bow, blue court shoes, cloth coat, handbag

Lose: suit jacket, bow from blouse, shoes

Add: cardigan, casual slip-on shoes, glasses

I.2: grey/blue suit skirt, blouse without bow, cardigan, casual slip-on shoes, (winter coat added during scene, onstage)

Interval

Introduction: cream blouse, brown/grey suit, blue court shoes, academic gown

Lose: academic gown, blue court shoes

Add: winter boots, red tam, red mitts, red scarf, winter coat, shoulder purse

II. 1: brown/grey suit, cream suit, red tam, red mitts, red scarf, winter coat, winter boots, shoulder purse

Lose: winter coat, mitts, tam, scarf, boots, purse

Add: glasses on chain, casual slip-on shoes

<u>II. 2</u>: brown/grey suit, cream blouse, casual slip-on shoes, glasses on chain

Lose: suit jacket, blouse, shoes

Add: blouse, blue court shoes, academic gown

<u>II. 3</u>: brown/grey skirt, blouse, academic gown, blue court shoes

Lose: academic gown

<u>Conclusion</u>: brown/grey skirt, blouse, blue court shoes

BOBBI ROY

I.2: blue smoking jacket, cream pants, Hawaiian shirt, sneakers, socks

Interval

II.1: sweatshirt, black stirrup pants, socks
Lose: sweatshirt, pants
Add: grey pants, black booties, red shirt, grey jacket
II.2: red shirt, grey jacket, grey pants, black booties
Lose: grey jacket, black booties
Add: string tie, cardigan,loafers
II.3: cardigan, red shirt, grey pants, loafers

## PROPERTY PLOT

Furniture and Set Dressing
lectern

Living Room
sofa (2 seater)
arm chair
coffee table (3 - 4' x 18" wide)
end table
small rug
writing desk
swivel chair
hall stand (catch all) by front door
trees
wastepaper basket
lamp on end table
gooseneck lamp (comes from box)
2 wall lamps by desk
outdoor lamp
curtains (opened from offstage)
phone (non-practical)
fishing net, starfish, etc. - dressing for bar
nautical lamp
wall dressing - flying ducks, etc.
folding door on closet
dressing in closet

Office
desk
desk chair (swivel)

side chair
2 drawer filing cabinet
standing coat rack
wastepaper basket
desk dressing - in/out tray, pens, pencils, blotter, papers, etc.
wall of books
tea kettle on tray with coffee/tea making - spoon, napkins, cookies

Hand Props

I,1
cardboard boxes - one to be unpacked containing: sheafs of paper, pencils, piles of periodicals i.e. *Atlantic Monthly, Time*, favorite mug, lucky charm sculpture, etc.
1 box containing 12 bottles of scotch
2 large suitcases - one unpacked containing clothes, shampoo, alarm clock, toothpaste, etc.
portable typewriter in case (manual)
glasses for bar - mismatched, tray, (others to appear later)
book - *PAPERS* - read from, new with paper cover
pen (MYRA)

I,2
portable tape recorder in case
steno pad (MYRA)
file folder containing poems with text

II.1

briefcase (MYRA) - dressed including 1 or 2 books

draft of chapters of book (typed script)

II.2

serious book

Eliot essay (BOBBI) - front page written on

II.3

manuscript

mug of coffee

large looseleaf manuscript *PAPERS* - ratty

tray with plate of sandwiches and teapot and fixings

1 large vase of summer flowers

flowers outside window - flip up

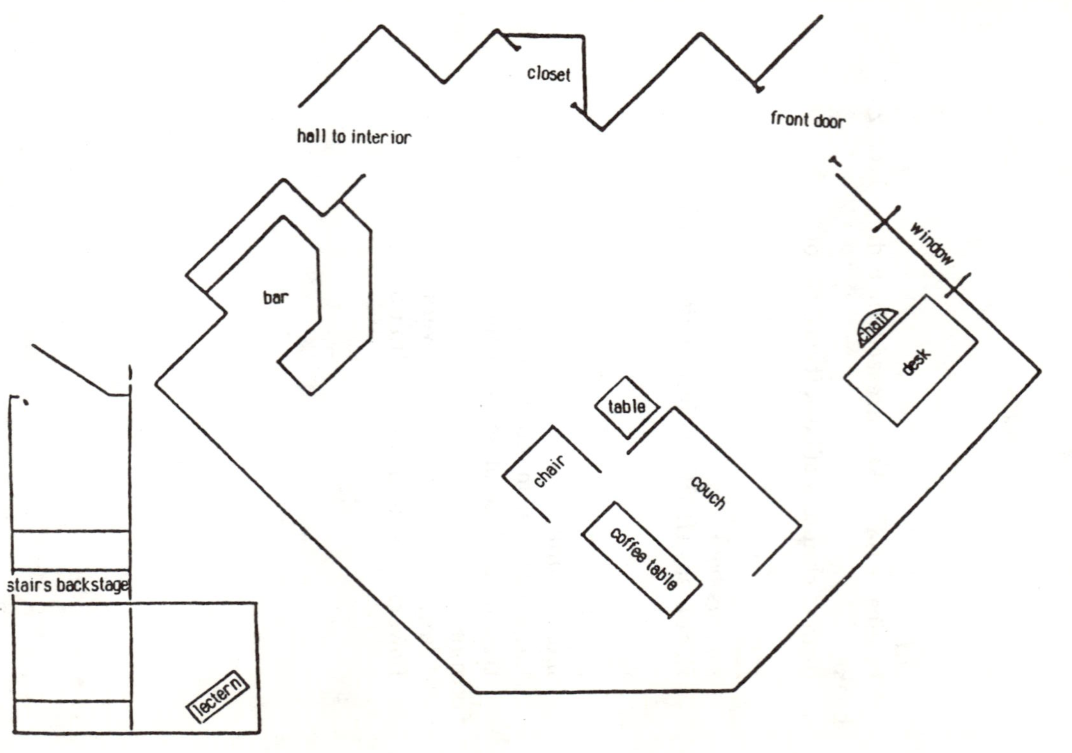


**PAPERS : set design by Iain Aitken**